The Slow Cooker Baki

A Hand Guide With Over 100 Fabulous New Recipes Cake, Pies, Fruit Desserts, and Much More

Teresa Moore

Copyright 2018

Your Free Gift

I wanted to show my appreciation that you support my work so I've put together a free gift for you.

[Smoothie Recipe Book:
200+ Perfect Smoothies Recipes for Weight Loss Detox, Cleanse and Feel Great in Your Body](#)

Just visit the link above to download it now.

I know you will love this gift.

Thanks!

Table of Contents:

Introduction

Corn porridge on milk

Pearl barley

Wheat porridge

Pumpkin country style

Pearl barley with chicken ventricles

Pearl barley with mushrooms

Pilaf with dried fruits

The Hungry Kutya

Pearl barley with pumpkin

Lentil porridge with meat and vegetables

Porridge "Peasant"

Millet porridge with poppy seeds

Pea porridge with pork

Monastic porridge

Buckwheat porridge with meat and mushrooms

Lentils with turkey and vegetables

Brown rice with meat and vegetables

Rice milk porridge

Buckwheat porridge with meat

Pilaf

Rice porridge with pumpkin

Rice porridge with quince

Potato and mushroom casserole

Zebra Pie

Chocolate cake with sour cream

Pork stewed with vegetables

Rassolnik

Beef Goulash

Meatballs

Cottage cheese casserole

Braised cabbage

Buckwheat porridge with meat

Chanakhi

Chicken Saltison

Honey pumpkin

Rice casserole with chicken

Borscht

Potato with chicken hearts

Soup with meatballs

Omelette with sausages

Eggs in the Slow cooker

Omelette in the multivariate

Fritatta with courgettes

Corn porridge

Semolina

Buckwheat with mushrooms

Buckwheat with sausages

Millet porridge with vegetables

Milk buckwheat porridge

Milk rice porridge

Ciabatta

Pie with pears on yogurt

Cherry pie

Cheese pie with chicken

Lime cake

Charlotte "Banana Paradise"

Pizza with mushrooms

Apple Charlotte

Lviv cheese list

Cake with plums and apples

White bread

Chocolate cake with sour cream

Cheese cake

Brownie on beer

Steamed Cheesecake

Curd cake with chocolate chip cookies

Cupcakes

Cupcake "Dark Night"

Carrot cake

Oatmeal pie with pears

Mannic from childhood

Coffee cupcake

- Bread at home
- Gingerbreads with chocolate filling
- Cake - pie
- Homemade pizza
- Cake on yogurt
- Pie with apples
- Pizza
- Charlotte with apples
- Cake
- Strudel from dumpling dough
- Fish pie
- Honey Biscuit
- Pie with meat
- Buns
- Cupcake with frozen blueberries and nuts
- Curd cake
- Orange pie in the Slow Cooker
- Cottage cheese casserole with berries
- Pancakes
- Casserole with spinach and cottage cheese
- Cheesecake with blueberries
- Pineapple cake
- Banana Cake
- Pie with cranberries in a multicrew
- Cake with strawberries
- Apple-honey cake
- Lemon cake
- Coconut cake

Introduction

Slow Cooker is an indispensable household appliance in the kitchen. Slow Cooker greatly simplifies the process of baking, shortens the time spent by the cooker, and gives an opportunity to realize useful and delicious recipes. With her help, even a beginner in the kitchen, turns into a chef, and easily learns not only simple baking recipes in a multivariate, but also outstanding culinary delights. Here you will find step-by-step recipes for refined dishes of confectionery art. Many baking recipes in the Slow Cooker are simple and simple, even an inexperienced mistress can easily implement them. By the choice of each of them we approached creatively, placed not only novelties, but also proven recipes. Cook with pleasure, and you will certainly be satisfied with the result.

Corn porridge on milk

Ingredients:
- 1 liter of milk
- 1 cup corn cereal
- butter
- a pinch of salt
- sugar

Preparation:
1. In a bowl Slow cooker pour rinsed corn crop, add salt, sugar and butter.
2. Pour in the milk and mix.
3. Switch on the "Milk porridge" mode and cook until ready.
4. Mix the porridge and serve it on the table. And you can leave the porridge in the "Heating" for another half an hour. During this time, it will thicken more strongly.
5. Serve the corn porridge hot. If desired, you can add raisins, dried apricots, nuts.

Pearl barley

Ingredients:
- 1 glass of pearl barley
- 250 g of meat
- 2.5 cups of water
- 1 carrot
- 1 onion
- 50 g of butter
- salt, spices

Preparation:
1. Cut the meat into slices and load into the pot Slow cooker.
2. Grate the carrots, cut the onions and put them on top of the meat.
3. Fall asleep, previously soaked for the night, pearl barley. Add salt, add your favorite spices, put butter. Fill with 2.5 glasses of water and turn the Slow cooker into the "Buckwheat"
4. All barley porridge is ready.

Wheat porridge

Ingredients:
- 1.5 cups of wheat flour
- butter
- 3 cups of water
- salt

Preparation:
1. We fall asleep in a pan of an Slow cookera of 1,5 cups of the washed-out groats and we fill in with 3 cups of water. Salt, add butter and turn on the "Buckwheat" mode.
2. Wheat porridge is ready.

Pumpkin country style

Ingredients:
- 300-400 g of pumpkin
- 0.5 cups of lentils
- 0.5 cups of rice
- 1 onion
- 50 g of vegetable oil
- salt

Preparation:
1. Peel the pumpkin, cut into cubes and lay on the bottom of the bowl.
2. Lentils and rinse with pumpkin. In the recipe was a green lentil and it must be cooked beforehand. But we like red lentils more. You do not need to boil it, it is boiled so quickly.
3. Put a layer of finely chopped onions on the lentils.
4. Rinse rice and put on a layer of onion. Add salt, oil, pour 1.5 glasses of water.
5. Cook in the mode of Pilaf / Kashi.
6. Mix the prepared dish and serve it hot on the table.

Pearl barley with chicken ventricles

Ingredients:
- 500 g chicken ventricles
- 200 g of pearl barley
- 1 onion
- 1 carrot
- salt, spices
- vegetable or butter

Preparation:
1. Pearl barley rinse, pour water and leave for several hours, you can at night.
2. Chicken ventricles should be cleaned of fat, cut into pieces of the desired size and rinsed thoroughly.
3. Chop the onion, grate the carrots or cut and fry in the oil in the bowl of the Slow cooker.
4. Add chicken ventricles to the fried vegetables.
5. With pearl barley, drain the water, in which it was soaked, and pour the rump into the bowl of the Slow cooker. Pour three glasses of water. Add salt, spices to taste.
6. Cook in the Pilaf / Kashi regime. Ready pearl porridge to mix.

Pearl barley with mushrooms

Ingredients:
- 1 glass of pearl barley
- 3.5 glasses of water
- 500 g of champignons
- salt pepper
- 1 onion
- vegetable oil

Preparation:
1. Rinse croup, pour water and leave for 6-8 hours, you can at night. To merge the water. Pour the groats into the bowl of the Slow cooker, pour 3.5 glasses of fresh water.
2. Finely chop onion and fry in vegetable oil.
3. Wash the mushrooms, cut into plates and add to the frying pan to the onions. Fry until the liquid evaporates.
4. Pour the onions and mushrooms into the bowl of the Slow cookera to the groats. Add salt, pepper. Cook on the Pilaf / Kasha.
5. Stir the porridge to mix.

Pilaf with dried fruits

Ingredients:
- 1 cup of rice
- 1 carrot
- dried apricots, prunes, raisins
- vegetable oil
- 0.5 teaspoon of salt
- barberry
- zira
- saffron

Preparation:
1. Dried fruits and rinse with hot water for swelling.
2. Cut the dried apricots and prunes into slices, leave whole raisins. Carrot cut into small cubes.
3. At the bottom of the pot, pour the vegetable oil and put into it dried fruit with carrots.
4. Rinse the rice and spread it over the carrots with dried fruits.
5. Salt and seasonings.
6. Pour 2-2,5 multi-glass hot water, the amount of water depends on the amount of dried fruits. If dried fruits are many, then more water will be needed. Water should lightly cover the rice, about 2 cm.
7. Turn on the "Pilaf" and wait for the ready signal.
8. Pilaf with dried fruits in the Slow cooker is ready.

The Hungry Kutya

Ingredients:
- 0.5 glass of pearl barley
- poppy
- dried fruits
- Walnut
- honey
- 3 liters of water
- 2 tablespoons honey
- 350-400 g of dried fruits

Preparation:
1. Pearl barley rinse, pour cold water and leave for several hours better at night. Boil the croup until ready, you can in the Slow cooker in the mode of porridge.
2. Poppy can be bought already ready, it should only be poured with boiling water.
3. Dried fruits with pour boiling water for a few minutes.
4. Brew the knot. For this, dry fruits thoroughly rinse, pour water and leave for half an hour. Drain the water in which dried fruits were soaked, pour three liters of cold water and put on a stove. Bring the tank to a boil, remove from the plate, cover and leave to infuse. When the knot has cooled to a warm state, add honey. Honey is added to the warm knot, not hot.
5. Add poppy, dried fruits, nuts and honey to the ready porridge. Mix. Pour the knot and serve.

Pearl barley with pumpkin

Ingredients:
- 150 g of pearl barley
- 400 ml of water
- 400 g of pumpkin flesh
- salt
- vegetable oil
- dried herbs or greens

Preparation:
1. Pour the pearl barley, pour into the cup Slow cooker, pour water and leave for a few hours to swell. You can leave for the night.
2. Then clean the pumpkin, cut into slices and add to the bowl Slow cookera to the pearl barley.
3. Add salt, dried herbs and mix. Cook in the Pilaf / Kashi / Buckwheat mode. In the finished porridge add the vegetable oil, mix.
4. Pearl porridge with pumpkin to serve on the table hot.

Lentil porridge with meat and vegetables

Ingredients:
- 300 g of meat
- 2 multi-lentils
- bow
- carrot
- 200 g of vegetables
- vegetable oil
- salt, spices
- 4 glasses of water

Preparation:
1. Onions, carrots and meat fry in vegetable oil in the "Bake" mode for 10-20 minutes.
2. Add any cut vegetables.
3. Then fall asleep laced rubbish.
4. Fill with 4 multi-glasses of water. Add salt, add spices at will.
5. Cooking in the "Pilaf".
6. Lentils cooked with mashed potatoes and porridge turned out very delicate and tasty.

Porridge "Peasant"

Ingredients:
- 1 cup of peas
- 1 glass of pearl barley
- 20-30 g of vegetable oil
- salt, spices
- 5 glasses of water

Preparation:
1. At the bottom of the bowl pour the chopped onions and carrots, add a piece of butter, in the post you can replace butter with vegetable.
2. Pour the pearl barley and peas with cold water and leave for several hours. Then drain the water, pour the rump and peas into the bowl.
3. Pour water, add salt and spices.
4. Cook in the "Pilaf" before the signal.
5. In the morning, a fragrant, nourishing hot "peasant" porridge was ready.

Millet porridge with poppy seeds

Ingredients:
- 1.5 cups of millet
- 4 glasses of milk
- sugar
- 1 tablespoon honey
- 25 g of butter
- 0.5 teaspoon of salt
- 0,5 cup dry poppy

Preparation:
1. Millet rinse, pour into the bowl Slow cookera, add salt, sugar and butter.
2. Pour the millet with milk.
3. Cook on the "Buckwheat".
4. Mack wash in warm water, then crush in mortar. Add honey and 50 ml of milk. Stir and pour into a ready warm porridge.
5. If there is a poppy filling, then dilute half the portion in milk and pour into the porridge.
6. Stir.
7. Kasha can be decorated with berries, pieces of fruit, jam.

Pea porridge with pork

Ingredients:
- 500 g of pork
- 2 onions
- 1 cup dried pea
- 1 cup of water or broth
- vegetable oil
- salt, pepper, spices
- greenery

Preparation:
1. Cut the meat into small pieces and fry in vegetable oil in the Baking / Frying mode, about 15 minutes.
2. During this time, chop the onion and add to the meat. Fry for another 5 minutes.
3. Then peas, pre-washed, add to the bowl Slow cookera to the meat. Add salt, pepper, spices and pour hot water or broth.
4. Cook in the quenching mode for about 1.5 hours, until the water boils and the peas are not boiled in mashed potatoes. If the liquid remains a lot, and the peas are already boiled, you can turn on the Baking / Frying mode for a few minutes. In this mode, intense boiling will begin. Caution when opening the cover!
5. Sprinkle the dish with greens before serving.

Monastic porridge

Ingredients:
- 1/3 cup of rice
- 1/3 cup of buckwheat
- 1/3 cup pearl barley
- 2 cups of water
- salt
- vegetable oil
- 1 onion
- 100-200 g of champignons

Preparation:
1. Cut the onions and mushrooms and save them in butter in the Baking / Frying mode. Fast cooking.
2. Pearl barley soak in advance for a couple of hours. Then, push aside the onion and mushrooms, pour the pearl barley into the bowl.
3. Pour the washed rice onto the pearl barley.
4. Pour the last washed layer of washed buckwheat.
5. Pour hot water, salt.
6. Cook in the mode of Quenching or Milk porridge 1 hour. Stir the porridge in the bowl.

Buckwheat porridge with meat and mushrooms

Ingredients:
- 300 g of meat flesh
- 150 g of mushrooms
- salt pepper
- 1 cup of buckwheat
- 1.5 cups of water
- vegetable oil

Preparation:
1. Pour the oil into the bowl of the Slow cooker oil. Switch on the "Baking" mode. Cut the meat and send to the bowl Slow cooker.
2. Mushrooms chopped and added to meat.
3. After 10 minutes, pour rinsed buckwheat, pour hot water, salt, pepper. You can do without pre-roasting.
4. Switch the Slow cooker to the "Pilot" mode. You can cook and on the "Buckwheat". After the signal, the ready porridge mixes and serve on the table, refilling if desired, butter.

Lentils with turkey and vegetables

Ingredients:
- turkey - 350-400 g
- lentils - 350 g
- vegetables - 300-400 g
- garlic
- salt

Preparation:
1. Finely chop turkey and lay on the bottom of the bowl Slow cooker.
2. Cut and put on top of vegetables, lentils and pour water.
3. Add salt and add garlic.
4. Cook in the Slow cooker in the mode "Pilaf" 1 hour.

Brown rice with meat and vegetables

Ingredients:
- 300-400 g of meat
- 2 cups brown rice
- 4-4.5 glasses of water
- frozen vegetables
- vegetable oil
- salt pepper
- barberry, spices

Preparation:
1. Wash meat and cut into pieces. In a bowl Slow cooker pour vegetable oil and load it into the meat.
2. Rinse brown rice, pour water and leave overnight. Before the finished water with rice pour off and rice to fall asleep in the Slow cooker.
3. Pour the vegetables onto the rice.
4. Add salt, pepper, spices, condiments.
5. Fill with water. Cook on the "Pilaf".
6. Mix the rice.
7. Serve brown rice with meat and vegetables hot, with heat and heat.

Rice milk porridge

Ingredients:
- 0.5 multi-cup rice
- 3 cup milks
- 0.5 teaspoon salt
- sugar
- 1 tablespoon butter

Preparation:
1. Rinse rice and pour into the pot Slow cooker.
2. Pour rice with cold milk. If you want, that porridge was rarer, increase the amount of milk or take less rice, but make sure that the milk level was below the maximum. Add salt, sugar and butter.
3. Select "Milk porridge" mode in the menu.
4. After the end of cooking, let stand in the "Heating" mode for 5 minutes and rice milk porridge can be served on the table.

Buckwheat porridge with meat

Ingredients:
- 2 cups buckwheat groats
- 4 glasses of water
- 300g of any meat
- 1 carrot
- 1 onion
- salt
- butter
- Spice

Preparation:
1. Place a piece of butter on the bottom of the Slow cooker bowl. Cut the meat into small pieces. On the oil lay out pieces of meat, distributing evenly on the bottom of the pan.
2. Cut the onion into small cubes. Carrots grate and place onions and carrots on meat.
3. Rinse the buckwheat. Place on top of carrots and onions. Add salt and spices to taste.
4. Add water to 4 multi-cups. Turn the Slow cooker on the "Pilaf" mode.
5. Mix the buckwheat with the meat in the Slow cooker. The dish must be served hot.

Pilaf

Ingredients:
- 300 g of pork
- 1 cup of rice
- 1 carrot
- 1 onion
- 2 cups of water
- spice
- salt
- vegetable oil

Preparation:
1. Cut pork into portions
2. Finely chop onion.
3. Grate the carrots.
4. At the bottom of the pot, pour a little vegetable oil, then spread the meat, on top of it onions and carrots.
5. Pour out and level the rice on a saucepan.
6. Add salt, pepper, add your favorite seasonings.
7. Fill with two cups of water and turn the Slow cooker on the "Pilaf"
8. The Slow cooker squeaks, then the pilaf is ready.

Rice porridge with pumpkin

Ingredients:
- 1 cup of rice
- 3 cups of milk
- 300-400 g of pumpkin
- 1.5 tablespoons sugar
- 0.5 teaspoon of salt
- 25 g butter

Preparation:
1. Pumpkin to peel, cut into cubes and put into Slow cooker.
2. Given it's not very successful experience last time with a pumpkin, I decided to separately blow it out with butter on the "baking" mode for 15 minutes.
3. Then rinse the croup and add to the pumpkin.
4. Pour milk, add salt, sugar and mix.
5. That milk "did not run away" it is necessary to grease with the butter of the edge of the cup of the Slow cooker.
6. Cook on the "Milk porridge". Try the pumpkin, if it is ready, then mix and serve. If the pumpkin is firm, then you can add a little milk and turn on the "Quenching"
7. Instead of rice, you can take millet cereals. Rice porridge with pumpkin in the Slow cooker is ready.

Rice porridge with quince

Ingredients:
- 1 cup of rice
- 2-3 quinces
- 3 cups of water
- 70 g raisins
- 3 tablespoons sugar
- butter

Preparation:
1. Wash thoroughly, remove the core and cut into pieces.
2. Rinse the rice and pour it on the quince, add the washed raisins, sugar, if desired, butter.
3. Pour water into the bowl and turn on the Kasha / Pilaf mode. Cooking time approx. 60 minutes.
4. Stir the porridge to mix.
5. Serve rice porridge with a quince warm.

Potato and mushroom casserole

Ingredients:
- 5 medium potatoes
- 2 eggs
- 300-500 g of mushrooms
- 2 large onions
- 1 carrot
- vegetable oil
- salt pepper
- sour cream

Preparation:
1. Peel the onion and cut into strips or half-rings, cut the mushrooms into 2-4 parts. Fry the mushrooms and onions in vegetable oil.
2. Peel potatoes and carrots and grate on a large grater or combine.
3. Combine potatoes, carrots, fried mushrooms with onions, add eggs, salt, pepper and mix.
4. Lubricate the bowl of vegetable oil with vegetable oil, put the prepared mass in it and lightly tamper with it.
5. Cook in the mode Baking 60-80 minutes. Ready casserole leaves in the bowl Slow cooker for 20-30 minutes, and then remove, turning the bowl on the set plate.
6. Serve the potato-mushroom casserole warm, watering sour cream.

Zebra Pie

Ingredients:
- 3 eggs
- 250-300 g of sugar
- 2 tablespoons with mayonnaise slide
- 150 g melted margarine
- 1 teaspoon of hydrated soda
- 250 g of flour
- 2 tablespoons cocoa
- vegetable oil

Preparation:
1. Eggs beat up with sugar, add mayonnaise, slaked soda, melted margarine, flour and mix well. Divide the dough into two parts and add cocoa powder to one and mix.
2. Grease the pan of the Slow cooker oil with vegetable oil and spread a tablespoon into the center of the pan alternately: a white dough, on top of it a dark dough, and again white. It will blur in striped circles.
3. The top of the pie can be decorated with a toothpick. Bake in "Baking" mode until ready, about 80 minutes.
4. Baking time can vary, depending on the power of the Slow cooker.
5. Ready pie can be sprinkled with powdered sugar, and you can lubricate with cream or jam. You can also cut the cake into several cakes and lubricate them.

Chocolate cake with sour cream

Ingredients:
- 1 egg
- 180 g of sugar
- 250 ml of fatty sour cream
- 160 g of flour
- 3 teaspoons of cocoa powder
- 1 teaspoon of soda

Preparation:
1. Smooth the sour cream with sugar and egg until smooth.
2. Add the sifted flour, soda and cocoa powder. Thoroughly mix everything.
3. Grease the pan with a butter. Pour out the dough.
4. Bake in "Baking" mode or in the oven at a temperature of 180 degrees 40 minutes.
5. Remove the cooked pie with a steaming tray. Lightly cool.
6. Then wrap the cake in a food film and leave to cool completely. So, the cakes will be moister.
7. Chocolate pie on sour cream in Slow cooker is ready!

Pork stewed with vegetables

Ingredients:
- 700 g of pork
- 2 large tomatoes
- 2 onions
- 2 eggplants
- 2 small zucchinis
- 2 carrots
- 2 Bulgarian peppers
- salt pepper
- Vegetable oil
- Garlic
- Chili
- 100 g of butter
- Spices, herbs

Preparation:
1. Cut the meat into large pieces. In a bowl Slow cooker pour a little vegetable oil and put in it slices of meat. Fry the meat before changing the color in the Baking / Frying mode. Add salt, pepper and mix.
2. Peel carrots and cut into small pieces.
3. Cut the onions, you can half rings, you can finely.
4. Cut the eggplant into cubes.
5. Cut the marrows into cubes, cut the tomatoes into cubes.
6. Sliced vegetables lay on the meat layers: carrots, onions, eggplants, tomatoes, zucchini. The last layer is chopped Bulgarian pepper. If desired, you can add chopped chili. Place pieces of butter on top of vegetables.
7. Extinguish in the quenching mode for 1.5 hours without stirring. Mix the prepared dish and serve it hot on the table.

Rassolnik

Ingredients:
- 500 g of meat
- 0,5 multi-cup perlovki
- 1 large potato
- 1 large carrot
- 1 medium onion
- 2 large salted cucumber
- 2 tablespoons of tomato paste
- 0.5 cup cucumber brine
- salt pepper
- condiments

Preparation:
1. In the "Baking" mode, fry for 10 minutes in vegetable oil finely chopped onions and grated carrots. Then add sliced salted cucumber and fry for another 10 minutes.
2. We put in the meat, soaked in the evening with a pearl barley and potatoes.
3. Fill broth or hot water to the mark. Add salt, pepper, add cucumber pickle, tomato paste and seasonings. We cook in the "Quenching" mode for 2 hours.

Beef Goulash

Ingredients:
- Beef - 400 g
- Onion - 1 piece of medium size
- Tomato paste - 100 g
- Vegetable oil - 70 ml
- Garlic - 3-4 pieces
- Water - 1 glass
- Sweet pepper - 1 piece
- Salt
- Spice

Preparation:
1. Prepare the ingredients. The oil can be used as olive, as well as sunflower.
2. Meat well, dry and cut into cubes.
3. Chop the peppers.
4. Cut the onions.
5. Press the garlic.
6. Take the spices to your liking.
7. We put everything in the bowl of the Slow cooker, add the tomato paste, olive oil and pour out the water.
8. Turn on the quenching mode and set it to 1.5 hours.

Meatballs

Ingredients:
- 500 g minced meat
- 1 cup of rice
- 1-2 onions
- salt, spices
- 2 tablespoons of tomato paste
- 2 tablespoons sour cream
- Bay leaf
- salt, black pepper ground
- 1 teaspoon sugar

Preparation:
1. In minced meat add chopped onion, boiled rice, salt, spices.
2. Stir thoroughly.
3. From the received mass to form meatballs.
4. Separately mix the water, tomato paste, sour cream, salt, sugar. It is better to take water in boiling water. Pour the meatballs.
5. Switch on the "Quenching" mode for 1 hour.
6. Meatballs in the Slow cooker can be served with any garnish, but you can and without it.

Cottage cheese casserole

Ingredients:
- 500 g cottage cheese
- 5 eggs
- 2/3 cup sugar
- 1 cup kefir
- 0.5 cups of semolina
- 1 teaspoon baking powder
- 1 bag of vanillin

Preparation:
1. Manco pour kefir and allow to swell for 20-30 minutes.
2. Separate yolks from proteins. Cottage cheese, yolks, baking powder, vanillin, combine and grind.
3. Whip the whites.
4. Add sugar and beat again into a firm foam.
5. To cottage cheese add the mango with kefir and mix.
6. Just as neatly and slowly enter the curdled mango enter squirrels and mix.
7. Lubricate the multicast with butter.
8. Put the mass in the pan of the Slow cooker.
9. Bake for 40 minutes, then leave to warm for 50 minutes, then turn off the cartoon and do not open the lid for another 10 minutes.
10. Then remove the curd casserole with a steaming tray.

Braised cabbage

Ingredients:
- cabbage
- salt
- condiments
- tomato paste
- vegetable oil
- frozen "Mexican mixture"

Preparation:
1. Lubricate the pot of the Slow cooker with vegetable oil, pour out the chopped cabbage. Salt, pepper, sprinkle with spices. Add a little water and put the "Quenching" mode for 45 minutes. You can cook and on the "Baking", but then the cabbage will not be so juicy
2. Then add the Mexican mixture. And put in the "Bake" mode for 20 minutes.
3. Then add the tomato paste, mix it and still in the "Baking" mode for 10-20 minutes.
4. Everything, Braised cabbage in the Slow cooker is ready.

Buckwheat porridge with meat

Ingredients:
- 2 cups buckwheat groats
- 4 glasses of water
- 300 grams of any meat
- 1 carrot
- 1 onion
- salt
- butter
- spice

Preparation:
1. Place a piece of butter on the bottom of the Slow cooker bowl. Cut the meat into small pieces. On the oil lay out pieces of meat, distributing evenly on the bottom of the pan.
2. Cut the onion into small cubes. Carrots grate and place onions and carrots on meat.
3. Rinse the buckwheat. Place on top of carrots and onions. Add salt and spices to taste.
4. Add water to 4 multi-cups. Turn the Slow cooker on the "Pilaf" mode.
5. Mix the buckwheat with the meat in the Slow cooker. The dish must be served hot.

Chanakhi

Ingredients:
- 500 g of pork
- 3 tomatoes
- 1 onion
- 400 g of potatoes
- 1 small eggplant
- 1 sweet Bulgarian pepper
- 4 pieces of garlic
- 25g butter
- salt pepper
- chopped greens

Preparation:
1. Cut the meat in large pieces, salt, sprinkle with your favorite seasoning and put it in Slow cooker.
2. Make a cross on a tomato cross, cross with boiling water and peel.
3. 1 cut the tomato and add to the meat, the other two cuts and set aside. Close the lid and put on "Quenching" for 1 hour.
4. Prepare the filling for the eggplant. Greens and garlic finely chopped, put into a bowl, add chopped finely 1 onion, salt, pepper, spices for any meat, butter slices, mix.
5. Cut the eggplant into 2 pieces across, and then cut the half along, but not to the end. In each incision to enclose the filling.
6. Cut the onion into strips, and pepper into large pieces.
7. After the meat is extinguished for about an hour, add the vegetables to it in layers: first the potatoes cut into large pieces.
8. Then onions, stuffing for eggplant, if left, pepper.
9. The last lay out the eggplant and the remaining tomatoes, cut into 4 parts. Salt-pepper to taste. Turn on "Quenching" for an hour again.
10. After an hour, if there is a lot of liquid, you can turn on the "Baking" mode and leave the Slow cooker cover open. 20 minutes will suffice. so that the liquid boils a little.
11. When ready, mix everything in a saucepan and sprinkle abundantly with different greens.

Chicken Saltison

Ingredients:
- 1,5 - 1,8 kg of chicken
- 25g gelatin
- salt, bell pepper
- Bay leaf
- garlic

Preparation:
1. Wash the chicken and cut into pieces. Fold the chicken, bay leaves, black peppercorns, into the Slow cooker, add salt and pour the chicken meat with gelatin, so that it is on all pieces of meat. Do not add water to the pan. Cook on the "Quenching" mode for 3 hours.
2. Then take out the chicken and cool it. Chicken the meat into pieces, removing the bones and skins. Grind the garlic and mix with chicken.
3. In the prepared form, tightly lay pieces of meat and pour juice, separated from the chicken, having previously strained it.
4. Chicken saltison completely cool, and then put in the refrigerator until completely hardened.

Honey pumpkin

Ingredients:
- 500 g of pumpkin
- 3 tablespoons honey
- cinnamon
- butter

Preparation:

1. Peel the pumpkin, cut into cubes. Pumpkin mixed with three tablespoons of honey and cinnamon. Pour a bowl of Slow cooker oil on butter and lay a pumpkin.
2. Switch on the "Baking" mode for 30 minutes.

Rice casserole with chicken

Ingredients:
- 1 cup of rice cereal
- 400 g of chicken ground meat
- 2 onions
- 1 carrot
- vegetable oil
- 2 eggs
- 3-4 tablespoons of sour cream
- salt, pepper, spices

Preparation:
1. Rinse one glass of rice and boil until cooked.
2. Finely chop the onion, grate the carrot and grate it in vegetable oil until soft.
3. Add the forcemeat, stir and fry 10-15 minutes.
4. Combine rice, minced meat with onions and carrots, eggs, sour cream, salt, pepper and spices.
5. Stir thoroughly.
6. Lubricate the bowl of the Slow cooker oil with vegetable oil and lay out the mass and level with a spatula. Bake in the baking mode 60-80 minutes.
7. Cook the casserole in a switched off Slow cooker for 15-20 minutes, then remove it from the bowl.

Borscht

Ingredients:
- water
- 300 g of meat
- 1 small beet
- 1 onion
- 1 carrot
- 2 potatoes
- 200 g cabbage
- 2 pieces of garlic
- tomatoes or 1 tablespoon of tomato paste
- vegetable oil
- greenery
- spices, salt, pepper

Preparation:
1. Pour a little vegetable oil on the bottom of the pot. Cover the saucepan with chopped onions and grated carrots. Fry in the "Baking" mode for 10-15 minutes.
2. Onions with carrots are fried. We put in a Slow cooker over carrots cut into small pieces of meat.
3. For the meat, we fall asleep grated beets. If you do not want it to lose its color when cooking, sprinkle it with lemon juice or vinegar. We put the cut potatoes on the beets.
4. Then put the shredded cabbage on the potatoes, squeeze out the garlic.
5. Add tomato paste, salt, pepper, seasoning.
6. Fill with hot boiled water and turn on the "Quenching" mode for 40 minutes. Preparedness can also depend on the variety of potatoes.
7. And by habit, after the "Quenching" mode for another 10 minutes "Baking", so that the borsch boiled. On the "Quenching" mode, he was just languishing.
8. Greens can be added before the end of cooking or straight into the plates. Let it brew for 20 minutes and serve hot with sour cream.

Potato with chicken hearts

Ingredients:
- 1.5 kg of potatoes
- 500 g of chicken hearts
- 2 onions
- 3 tablespoons sour cream 18%
- 100 ml of cream 18%
- salt pepper
- greenery
- vegetable oil

Preparation:
1. On vegetable oil fry the chopped onion until redness (in my cartoon - "Slow cooker 130" mode, but also "Hot" or "Baking").
2. Then add the chicken hearts to the onions and fry them from all sides.
3. Add the diced potatoes, add a little bit of water and simmer until the potatoes are soft in the "Quenching" mode.
4. Add sour cream and cream, add salt and pepper, mix.
5. Stew for another 10-15 minutes.
6. When serving decorate with greens.

Soup with meatballs

Ingredients:
- forcemeat
- potatoes
- carrot
- bow
- vegetable oil
- a tomato
- greenery

Preparation:
1. Finely chopped onions and grated carrots, put in Slow cooker. Add a little vegetable oil and turn on the "Bake" mode for 20 minutes. You cannot cover the lid.
2. Then add the tomato juice. And in the "Bake" mode 5 minutes.
3. Their meat minced balls of meatballs.
4. Pour water into the pan, better boiling water, and pour out the meatballs.
5. In the "Baking" mode, cook for 30 minutes, then add the diced potatoes and turn on the "Quenching" mode for 1 hour. It is possible and, in a mode, "Baking". but then it will boil strongly. Minutes for 10 before the end of cooking salt, add seasoning.
6. Soup with meatballs ready.

Omelette with sausages

Ingredients:
- eggs - 4 pieces
- milk - 150-200 ml
- sausages - 2 pieces
- cheese - 50 g
- onion - 1 piece
- butter
- salt, pepper, greens

Preparation:
1. Turn the Slow cooker on the "Bake" mode. In butter, fry onions, until golden, add sausage. Beat eggs with milk, salt and pepper. Pour this mixture into the Slow cooker. Pour out the diced cheese. We close the cover of the Slow cooker.
2. After 10-15 minutes, everything is ready.

Eggs in the Slow cooker

Ingredients:
- eggs of chicken
- salt
- butter

Preparation:
1. Pour 500 ml into the bowl of the Slow cooker. hot water, insert the steam tray. In the pallet put silicone molds, oiled, the number of eggs. In the molds, gently hammer eggs. Salt.
2. Switch on steam cooking mode for 15-20 minutes. If desired, simultaneously with the preparation of eggs, you can boil sausages in the bowl.
3. Serve eggs directly in the molds and eat them with a spoon.
4. And you can take out of the molds and serve with sauce, mayonnaise, sausages or vegetables.

Omelette in the multivariate

Ingredients:
- 1 - 1.5 tablespoons of flour
- 200 - 250 g of milk
- 5-6 raw eggs
- pinch of soda
- salt
- butter

Preparation:
1. Cover the flour with a ladle or a glass of a blender.
2. Slowly adding milk, blend a homogeneous mixture with a blender.
3. I started with a ladle and continued in the glass of the blender - the product does not fly out of it when whipped.
4. Add raw eggs to the mixture. Sprinkle salt and baking soda and beat until smooth.
5. Grease the pan with a butter and pour the resulting mixture.
6. Switch the Slow cooker to the "Baking" mode for 25 minutes. After finishing the baking, turn off the heating and do not open the Slow cooker for 5 to 10 minutes, to avoid omelet settling.

Fritatta with courgettes

Ingredients:
- 4 eggs
- 50 g cheese
- 1 vegetable marrow
- 1 sweet pepper
- salt pepper
- vegetable oil

Preparation:
1. Pepper cut into cubes. Zucchini cut into cubes or circles.
2. Pour oil into the bowl of the Slow cookera and lay out the vegetables. Enable the "Baking" mode.
3. Fry the vegetables for a few minutes until they become soft.
4. Whisk eggs with a fork, add grated cheese, salt, pepper.
5. Pour the vegetables with the beaten egg.
6. Fry for another 5-10 minutes.

Corn porridge

Ingredients:
- 1 cup of corn cereal
- 1 tablespoon butter
- 2 cups of milk
- 3 cups of water
- 1 tablespoon sugar
- a pinch of salt

Preparation:

Add to the saucepan Slow cookera butter and cereals. Switch to Baking mode for 10 minutes. Then add salt, sugar, water and milk. Turn the Slow cooker into the "Milk porridge" mode. The porridge is cooked for about 2 hours. Ready porridge to mix. You can add a little cream, so the porridge will be even tastier. On heating it is better not to leave.

Semolina

Ingredients:
- 1 cup of mango
- 4 glasses of milk
- 2 cups of water
- 60 g of butter
- sugar, salt

Preparation:

Pour 4 cups of milk into the bowl of the multivariate. Add 2 cups of water. Put 30 g of butter. Pour out 1 cup of mango. Add salt, sugar and mix.

Slow cooker put on the "Porridge", the time of readiness is 25 minutes. After cooking, add 30 g of butter, let it leave, mix.

Buckwheat with mushrooms

Ingredients:
- 250 g of mushrooms
- 1 onion
- 2 tablespoons butter
- 3 tablespoons sour cream
- 2 cups of buckwheat
- salt pepper

Preparation:
1. Finely chop the onion and mushrooms. Add to the Slow cooker oil. Turn on the "baking" mode, add onions and mushrooms. Cook for 10 minutes.
2. Open the lid, stir. Add buckwheat, sour cream and 1 glass of water. Salt well and season with pepper.
3. Put in the "Pilaf". When the mode is turned off, mix well.

Buckwheat with sausages

Ingredients:
- 1 cup of buckwheat
- 300 g sausages
- 1 onion
- 2 tablespoons butter
- salt

Preparation:
1. Slow cooker include in the "bake". Add butter, chopped sausages and chopped onions.
2. Fry 10 minutes. Mix. turn off the "baking" mode.
3. Wash buckwheat and add to the Slow cooker. Turn on the "buckwheat" mode. Cook for about 40 minutes.

Millet porridge with vegetables

Ingredients:
- 1 cup of cookie
- 1 carrot
- 1 onion
- 2 pieces of garlic
- 1 Bulgarian pepper
- 2 tablespoons butter
- salt pepper
- fresh coriander or parsley

Preparation:
1. Grate it with boiling water, rinse well. Grate the carrot, chop the onion, chop the peppers into strips or slices.
2. In a saucepan Slow cookera add butter and vegetables. Turn on the "Fry" or "Baking" mode, fry the vegetables for 10 minutes. Then add the millet, stir and fry for another 5 minutes.
3. Add salt, pepper, chopped greens, 3 cups of water, mix. Enable the "Rice" or "Pilaf" mode, cook until the beep.

Milk buckwheat porridge

Ingredients:
- 1 cup buckwheat
- 1 glass of water
- 2 cups of milk
- 2-3 tablespoons of sugar
- salt
- 1 tablespoon butter

Preparation:
1. Rinse the buckwheat well. Put it in the Slow cooker. Add sugar, a pinch of salt and butter. Mix everything.
2. Pour water and milk.
3. Put in the "milk porridge".
4. When the mode is finished, open the lid, stir. It is possible to give to stand for 5 minutes on "heating".

Milk rice porridge

Ingredients:
- 100 g of rice
- 500 ml of milk
- salt and sugar
- butter

Preparation:
1. Rinse rice several times, until clear water, pour milk.
2. Add sugar and salt, mix thoroughly.
3. On the Slow cooker, set the "Kasha" mode to 30 minutes.
4. When the porridge is ready, add butter to taste.

Ciabatta

Ingredients:
- 180 ml of water
- 1 teaspoon dried yeast
- 1 tablespoon sugar
- 1 teaspoon of salt
- 250 g of flour
- vegetable oil

Preparation:
1. Combine yeast, sugar, salt, warm water, sifted flour and knead the dough.
2. Cover the dough with a food film or lid and leave for 12 hours.
3. After 12 hours stir the dough, from the edge to the center.
4. Cover with a food film and leave for 6 hours.
5. After the time has passed, put the dough on the work surface with flour and roll the dough like an envelope. To do so several times.
6. Lubricate the bowl of vegetable oil with vegetable oil and shift the dough into it, creasing it downwards. Close the Slow Cooker and leave the dough in the switched off Slow Cooker for 4 hours.
7. First, bake in the baking mode 80-90 minutes.
8. Then turn over and bake on the other side for about 15 minutes.

Pie with pears on yogurt

Ingredients:
- 160 g of flour
- 1 teaspoon baking powder
- 250 g of sugar
- 120 ml of kefir
- 60 ml of vegetable oil
- 3 eggs
- 8-10 g of vanilla sugar
- 4 pears
- powdered sugar
- butter

Preparation:
1. Beat the eggs with sugar. Add vegetable oil, kefir, sifted flour, baking powder, vanilla sugar and whisk all until smooth.
2. Lubricate the bowl of the Slow Cooker oil. From the parchment for baking, cut a circle equal to the diameter of the bottom of the bowl, lay it on the bottom of the bowl and lubricate with oil.
3. Wash pears, peel and seeds, cut into slices and lay them tightly against each other in circles on the bottom of the bowl.
4. Pour the dough on the pears and smoothen.
Bake in the Baking mode 60 minutes, you can check the readiness with a match.
5. Remove the cooked pie with a steaming tray, remove parchment, cool and sprinkle with powdered sugar.

Cherry pie

Ingredients:
- 250 flours
- 3 eggs
- 100 g of sugar
- 10 grams of vanilla sugar
- 15 g of a baking powder
- 70 g sour cream
- 400 g of pitted cherries
- vegetable oil

Preparation:
1. In a deep bowl, combine the flour, eggs, sour cream, sugar, vanilla sugar and baking powder.
2. Knead the dough.
3. Remove cherries from the cherries and drain the juice and add cherries to the dough. Mix gently.
4. Lubricate the bowl of the Slow Cooker oil with vegetable oil and put the dough into it.
5. Bake in the "Baking" mode for 1 hour. Baking time can be different, it depends on the model of the Slow Cooker. The finished pie is left in the Slow Cooker for 20-30 minutes, and then extracted using a pan for steaming.
6. Sprinkle with cherry pie powdered sugar and serve for tea.

Cheese pie with chicken

Ingredients:
- 300 g chicken fillet
- 3 eggs
- 100 g of hard cheese
- 200 g sour cream
- 220 g of flour
- 120 g of butter
- 3 teaspoons baking powder
- 1-2 teaspoons dried herbs
- 1 teaspoon curry
- salt

Preparation:
1. Chicken fillet wash, cut into small pieces, sprinkle curry and herbs, stir and leave to marinate for 10-15 minutes.
2. Whisk the eggs with salt.
3. Add soft butter, grated cheese, sour cream to the egg mass and mix.
4. Add the sifted flour with baking powder and mix thoroughly.
5. Lubricate the bowl of the Slow Cooker with butter and put the pieces of chicken on the bottom.
6. Put the dough on the fillet and smooth it.
7. Bake in the baking mode 60-80 minutes. Slightly cool the cake without taking out from the Slow Cooker, and then take it out with a basket for steaming and serve.

Lime cake

Ingredients:
- 200 g of flour
- 100 g of cold oil
- 50 g of sugar
- 1 egg
- 1 tablespoon of milk
- 2-3 limes
- 300 g condensed milk
- 2 eggs

Preparation:
1. Mix the flour and sugar.
2. Add pieces of cold butter and quickly rub everything into the crumb before the butter has time to melt.
3. Add the egg and milk and mix the dough. Long knead is not worth it, stop right after you have a resilient mass. Put the batter in the refrigerator for half an hour.
4. Squeeze out the lime juice, then add the zest to it.
5. Mix eggs, condensed milk and lime juice, so that the mass becomes homogeneous.
6. Put two strips of baking paper on the bottom of the Slow Cooker bowl. Then spread the dough on the bottom of the bowl, forming the sides.
7. Pour into the bowl lime filling and put the "Baking" mode for an hour. In a ready-made pie, the filling should look like an omelet. Cool the cake and gently pull it out of the Slow Cooker using strips of paper.

Charlotte "Banana Paradise"

Ingredients:
- ripe bananas - 2 pieces
- eggs - 2 pieces
- flour - 1 glass
- Butter - 100 g
- sugar - 1 glass
- soda - a half teaspoon

Preparation:
1. Take a high cup, pour out sugar into it and smash eggs there. Beat the mixer for 5-7 minutes.
2. Half a banana mash with a fork until a homogeneous mass is obtained. Add the resulting gruel into the knocked-down eggs with sugar and whisk a little, pour in the flour and soda. Whisk another 5 minutes and pour melted butter - again whisk, but now only a couple of minutes.
3. Lubricating the cup Slow Cooker butter, pour in the resulting dough and decorate the banana. We set the mode of "multipurpose" 120 degrees for 45-50 minutes. When the signal for the completion of the Slow Cooker operation sounds, let the charlotte cool down a little and extract it.

Pizza with mushrooms

Ingredients:

- 2 tablespoons ketchup
- Jar of mushrooms
- 2-3 tablespoons of sauerkraut
- 2 sausages or sausages
- 2 tablespoons of mayonnaise
- Slice of hard cheese
- Spice
- Vegetable oil

Preparation:

1. After we have thawed and rolled out the dough, we need to grease the bowl of the Slow Cooker with vegetable oil and only then put our dough there. We try to distribute ketchup evenly.
2. At the edges distribute sauerkraut, and in the center, we spread the cut mushrooms. Sprinkle all this beauty with spices.
3. Beautifully put the sausages cut into slices.
4. Gently distribute the mayonnaise on our pizza and sprinkle it evenly on the grated cheese rubbed on a large grater. Set the mode "pizza" for 30 minutes.
5. Our pizza is ready! Wait for about 15 minutes before transferring to a plate to lightly cool and harden.

Apple Charlotte

Ingredients:
- 5 eggs
- 1 cup of sugar
- 1 cup of flour
- 5-6 large apples
- a pinch of salt
- 1 teaspoon of soda
- butter
- powdered sugar

Preparation:
1. Eggs, salt, sugar, soda, slaked with boiling water, pour into the dishes.
2. Shake well with either a blender or a whisk.
3. Add the sifted flour.
4. Bring the mixture to good uniformity with the same coroner or blender.
5. Peel apples from peel and cores and cut into slices.
6. Pour the prepared apples into the dishes with the prepared mixture and mix well with a spatula.
7. Lubricate the bowl of the Slow Cooker oil. The resulting mixture is poured into a bowl and run the "Baking" mode.
8. Bake for 60 to 80 minutes.
9. Remove the resulting charlotte from the bowl, sprinkle with powdered sugar and serve for tea!

Lviv cheese list

Ingredients:
- 700 grams of home-made cottage cheese
- 150 g of sugar
- 5 eggs
- 1 lemon peel
- 50-100 g raisins
- 1 tablespoon of semolina
- 1 tablespoon cornstarch
- 120 g of butter
- 3 tablespoons milk
- 65 g of chocolate without filler

Preparation:
1. Cottage cheese to grind through a sieve or to crush any other way: in a combine, through a meat grinder, etc. Pre-extract the butter and eggs from the refrigerator.
2. Transfer the cottage cheese into a deep bowl and start whisking, adding a little sugar.
3. Then, whisking, take turns adding eggs.
4. Let the lemon burn with boiling water and remove the zest.
5. Add to the mass of raisins, starch, semolina and zest. Mix.
6. Add soft butter, stir.
7. Lightly grease the multi-wool pot with butter. Pour out the dough. Cook on the "Baking" mode, approximately 50-60 minutes. Then let the cheese cake cool and use a cooking pan to steam the cheese cake.
8. While preparing the icing, the cheese can be put in the refrigerator. So, the glaze will grasp faster.
9. Put milk and chocolate in a ladle and on medium heat, stirring constantly, bring to a homogeneous mass.
10. Drizzle the cheese cake with chocolate, clean in the refrigerator for 6 hours, you can at night!

Cake with plums and apples

Ingredients:
- 3 eggs
- 1 glass of sour cream
- 1 cup of sugar
- 1.5 - 2 cups of flour
- 1 teaspoon of soda
- a pinch of salt
- plums
- apples
- powdered sugar

Preparation:
1. Eggs beat into a whipping container, add sugar and beat with a mixer until the sugar dissolves completely. Add sour cream and whip a little.
2. After adding sifted flour and soda. Mix everything well so that there are no lumps.
3. Lubricate the bowl of the Slow Cooker oil or vegetable oil. And put all the dough in the bowl of the Slow Cooker.
4. The filling can be done after the preparation of the test, as preparation does not take much time. Wash apples and plums. Split the halves, removing the bones. Cut the apples into slices.
5. First in the dough to lay out slices of plums arbitrarily, and then in the intervals to expand the lobules of apples. Bake the pie in the "Baking" mode for 50 minutes.
6. Finished the pie with a toothpick. And leave in a bowl to cool off a little.
7. Then carefully remove from the bowl.

White bread

Ingredients:
- 300 ml of warm water
- 540 g of flour
- 2 tablespoons of sugar
- 50 g melted butter
- 1 teaspoon of salt
- 2 teaspoons dried yeast

Preparation:
1. Melt butter, sift flour. Combine all the ingredients and knead the soft dough. Cover the bowl with the test towel and put in a warm place for one hour.
2. After an hour the dough will rise, it is good to crumple and form a ball
3. Put the ball of dough into a bowl of Slow Cooker oil lubricated with vegetable oil. If baked in the oven, then on the bread you need to make incisions with a sharp knife.
4. Leave in the bowl for half an hour. You can briefly turn on the Heating mode. Lubricate the top of the bread with whipped egg yolk.
5. Bake in the baking mode 60-80 minutes. Put the bread on the grate, cover with a towel and allow to cool completely.

Chocolate cake with sour cream

Ingredients:
- 1 egg
- 180 g of sugar
- 250 ml of fatty sour cream
- 160 g of flour
- 3 teaspoons of cocoa powder
- 1 teaspoon of soda

Preparation:
1. Smooth the sour cream with sugar and egg until smooth.
2. Add the sifted flour, soda and cocoa powder. Thoroughly mix everything.
3. Grease the pan with a butter. Pour out the dough.
4. Bake in "Baking" mode or in the oven at a temperature of 180 degrees 40 minutes.
5. Remove the cooked pie with a steaming tray. Lightly cool.
6. Then wrap the cake in a food film and leave to cool completely. So the cakes will be more moist.

Cheese cake

Ingredients:
- 100 g of cheese
- 150 g of flour
- 2 tablespoons mayonnaise
- 1 tablespoon Provenian meals
- 3 eggs
- 1 teaspoon baking powder
- 80 g of butter
- greens if desired

Preparation:
1. Grate the cheese on grater.
2. Add eggs, grated chilled butter, Provencal herbs, mayonnaise, chopped greens. Mix.
3. Add the sifted flour with baking powder. Mix.
4. Lubricate the bowl of the Slow Cooker oil and put the dough into it. Align.
5. Bake in the "Baking" mode for 60 minutes. Ready cake to cool in the Slow Cooker with the lid open.

Brownie on beer

Ingredients:
- 160 g of flour
- 30 g of cocoa
- 4 eggs
- 100 g of chocolate
- 110 g of butter
- 125 dark beer
- 300-350 g of sugar
- vanilla sugar
- a pinch of salt

Preparation:
1. Mix salt, cocoa, flour.
2. Melt the butter.
3. Remove from heat. Add the chocolate and stir it with a spatula until the chocolate dissolves completely.
4. Pour 125 ml of beer, mix.
5. 4 eggs mixed with sugar and a bag of vanilla sugar.
6. Beat with a mixer until the mass brightens and increases in size.
7. Pour the chocolate-oil mixture in a thin trickle, continuing to beat with a mixer.
8. Next add dry ingredients, gently mix with whisk until smooth.
9. Grease the pan of the Slow Cooker oil.
10. Put the dough. Put on the "Baking" mode for 1 hour.
11. After the signal from the Slow Cooker, take out Brownie using a steam pan.
12. Cool the pie and serve for tea.

Steamed Cheesecake

Ingredients:
- 600 g cottage cheese
- 200 ml of sour cream
- 2 eggs
- 1 tablespoon of starch
- 2 teaspoons of cocoa
- 100 g of sugar
- a few drops of vanilla extract

Preparation:
1. All the ingredients except cocoa are sent to a bowl and beat well with a blender
2. We divide the mass into two parts into one, add cocoa and mix.
3. Take the form from the Slow Cooker, cover the bottom where the holes are a sleeve for baking. Now pour directly into the center 2 tablespoons of vanilla mixture, pour 2 tablespoons of chocolate mixture into the center of vanilla seven.
4. Pour until mixes run out in both bowls. Next, we pour water into the capacity of the Slow Cooker to the mark 4. We put the mold on the bowl from above. We include the Slow Cooker on the program "Steaming for a couple" for 30 - 40 minutes. We check the finished cheesecake so! After the end of the program, carefully remove the shape and let the cheesecake completely cool.

Curd cake with chocolate chip cookies

Ingredients:
- 2.5 tablespoons of bitter cocoa
- 200 grams of shortbread cookie
- 150 g of butter
- 500 g cottage cheese
- 200 g sour cream
- 2 eggs
- 140-150 g of sugar
- 15 grams of vanilla sugar
- 4 tablespoons of starch
- chocolate chip cookies

Preparation:
1. Combine the cookies with cocoa.
2. Grind in a blender.
3. Add butter at room temperature and knead well to allow butter, biscuits and cocoa to mix evenly.
4. Put a strip of parchment paper in the pan of the Slow Cooker.
5. Lay out the basis for the pie, form a "basket" for the future filling.
6. Separate the proteins from the yolks.
7. Yolks, starch, cottage cheese, sour cream, sugar, vanilla sugar to combine.
8. Stir until smooth.
9. Whip the whiskers into an elastic foam.
10. Put into a saucepan with curd mass.
11. Gently stir so that the proteins do not settle.
12. To lay out half of cottage cheese mass on a basis.
13. To decompose and slightly press the chocolate cookie.
14. Cover with the second part of the curd mass.
15. Bake in the Slow Cooker on the "Baking" mode for 75 minutes.
16. Give the curd cake completely cool in the Slow Cooker.

Cupcakes

Ingredients:
- Milk - 100 ml
- Egg - 1 piece
- Cocoa - 3 g
- Flour 150 g
- Sugar - 140 g
- Baking Powder - 1.5 teaspoons
- Sugar vanilla - 20 g

Preparation:
1. In a separate bowl, whisk the egg with sugar and vanilla sugar.
2. Next we send milk there, mix well. And then we pour in the flour and baking powder and again interfere to homogeneity.
3. And then divide the dough into two equal parts and add cocoa to one, mix it.
4. We distribute our dough on silicone molds. Pour the dough alternately with a tablespoon. Fill up to the top of the paper mold.
5. Our cupcakes are sent to the Slow Cooker, at the bottom we pour out not less than 0.5 liters of water, put on the cake cupcakes. Turn on the function of "steaming" and send for 25 minutes. After 20 minutes you can look and check the toothpick for readiness.

Cupcake "Dark Night"

Ingredients:
- 4 eggs
- 150 g of butter or margarine
- 1.5 multi-cup sugar
- 2 tablespoons cocoa
- 0.5 teaspoon of soda
- 1.5 multistage flour
- Vegetable or butter

Preparation:
1. Slice the butter of room temperature with sugar.
2. One by one, we introduce eggs. We pour soda. We mix everything thoroughly. We introduce sifted flour. Stirring.
3. Pour in the cocoa. Once again, we mix well.
4. Lubricate the bowl of the Slow Cooker oil, pour the dough into the bowl.
5. Cook in the BAKERY mode for 50 minutes. take out using a pan for steaming.

Carrot cake

Ingredients:
- carrots grated - 1 glass
- eggs of chicken - 2 pieces
- sugar - 1 glass
- flour - 1 glass
- Butter - 100 g
- salt
- cinnamon - 1 tablespoon
- baking powder - 1 sachet
- half a glass of raisins
- half a glass of nuts

Preparation:
1. Whisk the eggs, add sugar to them and continue to beat until a thick foam. The main thing is to beat the eggs very carefully, then our cake will turn out to be magnificent and airy.
2. Melt the butter, put the oil in the Slow Cooker and set the "Heating" mode.
3. Now take the raw carrots, rinse it, gently clean it and three on a greater. To the eggs add grated carrots, butter.
4. To the eggs add a pinch of salt and cinnamon, half a glass of raisins, half a glass of nuts. All the ingredients are thoroughly mixed.
5. Sift flour, mix with a baking powder and pour into a bowl with dough. Carefully mix everything, so that in the test there were not even the smallest lumps.
6. We move it to the already oiled pot of the Slow Cooker. Choose the "Baking" mode and set the time - 65 minutes.
7. After the baking is finished, we give the pie a little bit to stand in the Slow Cooker without opening the lid, after which carefully take out the pie and let it cool on the grate.

Oatmeal pie with pears

Ingredients:
- Oat flakes "Hercules" - 1,5 cups
- Sugar - 1 glass
- Vegetable oil - 3/4 cup
- Flour - 1 glass
- Soda - 1 teaspoon
- Salt - pinch
- Pear - 1,5 pieces

Preparation:
1. Mix sugar, salt, soda, vegetable oil.
2. Add oat flakes and flour.
3. Stirring.
4. Pear the crumb in a blender, add to the dough.
5. Lubricate the bowl of the Slow Cooker with vegetable or butter, pour the dough into the bowl.
6. Cook in the BAKING mode for one bowl.

Mannic from childhood

Ingredients:
- 2 cups of curdled milk
- 2 tablespoons honey
- 1 cup of mango
- 1 egg
- a pinch of salt
- 1.5 teaspoon soda
- 3 tablespoons butter
- 50-70 g raisins
- 50-70 g dried apricots
- 50-70 g prunes
- Cassel powder
- 2 cups of water

Preparation:
1. Thick not very acidic curdled milk mixed with honey, salt and a glass of mango. Leave for 2-3 hours. Then add the egg, soda. Mix all.
2. Smooth the Slow Cooker cream with butter, pour out the "dough" and top with 3 tablespoons of melted butter. Put on the "baking" for 30 minutes. Cool it down.
Brew the KISEL. Dried fruits pour water and cook for 5 minutes. If you use starch, then add sugar and a little citric acid, starch dilute 30-50 g of water and pour into a boiling short. Cook until thick.
3. Ready pudding chilled, cut into portions and poured with a cool acid.

Coffee cupcake

Ingredients:
- 1 cup of sugar
- 2 eggs
- 1.5 cups of flour
- 2 tablespoons mayonnaise
- 100 g butter or margarine butter
- 4 teaspoons instant coffee
- 0.5 teaspoon baking powder
- cinnamon powder
- vanilla sugar
- a pinch of salt

Preparation:
1. Mix sugar and eggs.
2. Stir and beat into foam.
3. Add flour. Stir in the softened margarine and mayonnaise. Knead the dough. Add baking powder, vanilla sugar, cinnamon, pinch of salt. Mix.
4. Dissolve coffee in a third of a glass of warm water.
5. Add coffee to the dough, mix.
6. If desired, add crushed nuts.
7. Grease the pan of the Slow Cooker oil.
8. Put the dough and put it on the "Baking" mode. Willingness to check with a toothpick.
9. Remove the ready-made coffee cake from the Slow Cooker.
10. Decorate the coffee cake with glaze, sprinkle with almond petals and serve for tea!

Bread at home

Ingredients:
- flour 0,5 kg
- yeast 1 teaspoon
- 1 teaspoon sugar
- salt
- 0.5 liters of water

Preparation:
1. In the flour, add yeast, salt, sugar, knead the dough to a homogeneous mass.
2. Lubricate the bowl with a sunflower oil, put the dough there, and put on the "Bread" mode for 5 hours, after 2.5 hours, turn the bread and leave until done.

Gingerbreads with chocolate filling

Ingredients:
- Butter - 1,5 tablespoons
- Egg - 1 piece
- Sugar - 0,5 cups
- Soda
- Flour - 2 cups
- Chocolate - 50 g

Preparation:
1. In the bowl, melt the butter.
2. Add the egg.
3. Add sugar. We mix it.
4. Do not forget about soda. Mix again.
5. Introduce the sifted flour, knead the dough.
6. From the dough piece, we form a cake, put a piece of chocolate in the center.
7. Form the ball so that the chocolate is inside. Such balls are formed from the whole test. We put them in a container-steamer. Pour boiling water into the cup of the Slow Cooker. Set the bowl, turn on the VARK ON PAIR mode for 30 minutes.
8. After the signal, put the gingerbread cookies on a plate.

Cake - pie

Ingredients:
- flour - 230 g
- chocolate black - 100 g
- walnut - 150 g
- cocoa - 20 g
- baking powder - 2 teaspoons
- sugar - 100 g
- salt - 1 teaspoon
- eggs - 3 pieces
- vegetable oil - 230 ml
- milk - 2 tablespoons
- 100 g of dark chocolate

Preparation:
1. Prepare the dough. Chop nuts and chocolate. Mix the flour with baking powder, cocoa, salt and vanilla. Whip the whipped beans and a half of sugar. Mix the yolks with the remaining sugar. Then the proteins are injected into the yolks. All this mixture alternately adds to the flour, then vegetable oil, and then milk. Mix all the dough with a mixer at medium speed. After the mixer in the dough, add chopped chocolate and nuts. Mix everything. The form should be oiled and baked at a temperature of 180 degrees for about 1 hour.
2. We take the finished pie from the Instant Pot and cool it.
3. Fill it with melted black chocolate.

Homemade pizza

Ingredients:
- Dough - 250 g
- Minced meat - 300 g
- Eggs boiled - 2 pieces
- Tomatoes - 2 pieces
- Cheese - 150 g
- Mayonnaise - 1 tablespoon
- Vegetable oil

Preparation:
1. Lubricate the bowl with vegetable oil. Dough roll in a thin circle, put in a bowl, form the sides.
2. Place the forcemeat on a smooth layer.
3. Salt, pepper, lightly grease with mayonnaise.
4. Eggs grate on a large grater, place on minced meat.
5. Put the next layer of tomatoes.
6. Sprinkle with grated cheese on a large grater.
7. Close the Slow Cooker cover, set the BAKING mode to 50 minutes. After the signal for cooking, you need to leave the pizza in the bowl for 15 minutes.

Cake on yogurt

Ingredients:
- 200 g of sugar
- 400 g of flour
- 100 g of butter
- 3 eggs
- 250 ml of kefir
- 10 g of a baking powder
- a pinch of salt
- 1 packet of vanilla sugar
- raisins, nuts

Preparation:
1. Beat eggs with sugar in a lather.
2. Add melted butter, kefir, salt, vanilla sugar. Mix.
3. Add the flour mixed with the baking powder and sifted. If desired, add raisins, nuts or prunes, dried apricots. Mix everything.
4. Lubricate the bowl of the Slow Cooker oil and pour the dough into it.
5. Bake in the "Baking" mode for about 60 minutes. Finished cake is extracted using a baking grid for steaming.

Pie with apples

Ingredients:
- 3 eggs
- 150-200 g of sugar
- 200 g of flour
- 0.5 teaspoon of soda
- 3-4 apples

Preparation:
1. Mix all the ingredients. The dough is divided in half. One-part pours into the bowl Slow Cooker.
2. Peel the apples and rub them gently on a coarse grater so that the juice does not flow. Gently, pour the apple shavings onto the dough and top with a second half of the dough. Put the Slow Cooker for 40-45 minutes on top of the ready-made and cooled pie can be sprinkled with powdered sugar or each chopped piece of decorated with whipped cream.

Pizza

Ingredients:
- 1 teaspoon dried yeast
- 1 teaspoon of salt
- 2 teaspoons of sugar
- 3 tablespoons vegetable oil
- 0, 5 cups of water
- 1.5 cups of flour
- boiled chicken fillet
- pork balyk
- hard cheese
- Champignon
- tomato sauce

Preparation:
1. Mix flour, water, yeast, vegetable oil, salt and sugar into an elastic dough.
2. Cover with a towel or food film and leave to go for 1-1.5 hours.
3. For the filling: chicken fillet, balyk and champignons cut into pieces. Cheese three for a large grater.
4. Approach the dough lightly to crumple, divided into two parts. One part of the kneading hands, giving it the shape of a circle, the size of a little more than the bottom of the bowl.
5. Lubricate the dough with tomato sauce.
6. And lay out the layers of stuffing: cheese, chicken fillet, balyk, mushrooms and again cheese. If you want, you can grease the top of the pizza with mayonnaise.
7. Bake in the "Baking" mode for 40 minutes. With the second part of the test, do the same.

Charlotte with apples

Ingredients:
- 3 eggs
- 1 cup of sugar
- 1 cup of flour
- 1.2 teaspoons of soda
- 4-5 apples

Preparation:
1. Beat the egg mixer and sugar. Add the flour, mix. Add the soda. Cut the apples.
2. Lubricate the silicone mold with oil, sprinkle with breadcrumbs, put apples on the bottom, put dough on top.
3. Put in the Slow Cooker, turn on the "Baking" mode for 50 minutes. After the Slow Cooker enters the heating mode, turn it off, open the lid, let the cake cool down a little.

Cake

Ingredients:
- 3 eggs
- 250 g of sugar
- 250 g of flour
- 125 ml of milk
- 150 ml of vegetable oil
- 100 g of ground nuts
- 1 bag of baking powder
- 1 packet of vanilla sugar
- 3 tablespoons sugar for sprinkling

Preparation:
1. Whip eggs with sugar.
2. Add milk, vanilla sugar, flour, baking powder and mix. Then pour in the vegetable oil and mix thoroughly until smooth.
3. Grease the pan of the Slow Cooker and pour the dough into it.
4. Nuts chop, mix with sugar and sprinkle the top of the cake.
5. Bake in "Baking" mode for 40 minutes, then turn over and another 20 minutes on the other side.

Strudel from dumpling dough

Ingredients:
- meat-300 - 400 g
- potatoes 500 - 600 g
- onions - 1 piece
- pastry dough - 300 g
- Butter - 80 g
- salt pepper
- seasonings and bay leaves

Preparation:
1. Fill the meat with water. The water is enough 400-500 ml. That the meat was covered with water.
2. Turn the Slow Cooker on the "Soup" mode.
3. We roll the dough thinly, grease the melted butter and turn into a roll. Roll cut into rolls 3 cm wide.
4. Meat is cooked, we take it from the broth and cut into portions, we return it back to the broth. To the meat, add the peeled potatoes, cut into large bars and chopped onion, salt, seasonings, bay leaf.
5. Putting out strudel. The main thing: there should not be a lot of water, it should not cover potatoes with meat. We close the Slow Cooker and turn on the "Cabbage rolls" mode.
6. After 20 minutes your dish will be ready!

Fish pie

Ingredients:
- flour
- 1 teaspoon dry yeast
- 150 ml of fermented baked milk
- salt
- 1 onion
- 1 glass of pink salmon
- 1 potato
- pepper black ground
- salt

Preparation:
1. Combine the flour, salt, yeast and fermented baked milk and knead the dough. Flours are necessary so much that the soft elastic dough, approximately 300 was received. And to leave in a warm place to approach.
2. Prepare the filling. To do this, drain the liquid from the canned food and mash it with a fork. Add the chopped onion and finely chopped raw potatoes. I cut the potatoes with a knife to clean vegetables, very thin plates were made. Fill with salt, pepper and mix.
3. Grease the pan of the Slow Cooker oil. The dough is divided into two parts. One part to lay on the bottom of the Slow Cooker. For the dough to fill stuffing.
4. The filling is covered with the second half of the dough, we patch the edges and pierce the top with a fork.
5. Bake in the "Baking" mode for 40-60 minutes. Then turn over and still bake for 10-15 minutes. Extract the fish cake from the Slow Cooker with a steaming tray.

Honey Biscuit

Ingredients:
- 6 tablespoons honey
- 1 cup of sugar
- 1 teaspoon of soda
- 2-2.5 cups of flour
- 5 eggs

Preparation:
1. Mix eggs and sugar with a mixer.
2. Separately, melt the honey + soda until the honey becomes dark, cool a little.
3. Gradually introduce honey into the egg mixture
4. Then add the flour.
5. Put the finished dough in the pre-oiled bowl of the Slow Cooker. Bake 45 + 15 minutes. Sponge cake with a basket from the steamer, cool, cut into cakes and soak with your favorite cream.

Pie with meat

Ingredients:
- 300 g of wheat flour
- 250 ml of milk
- 3/4 teaspoon of salt
- 40 g butter
- 1 tablespoon vegetable oil
- 1 teaspoon dried yeast
- 300 g minced meat
- 1 onion
- salt pepper
- 2 tablespoons of broth or boiled water

Preparation:
1. We combine all the ingredients for the dough and mix not very steep dough.
2. Cover with a towel or food film and leave for 30-40 minutes in a warm place.
3. Add minced onion, salt, pepper, broth to the stuffing and stir.
4. Lubricate the bottom of the pan with vegetable oil. The dough is divided into two unequal parts. 2/3 parts of the dough lining the bottom of the pan. making the skirts. And 1/3 of the test is left.
5. Lay the forcemeat on the dough, level it.
6. Cover the forcemeat with the remaining one third of the dough and pat the edges. Turn on the "Heating" mode for 20 minutes.
7. Then turn on the "Baking" mode for 65 minutes.
8. When finished, turn and bake for another 20 minutes. The signal will indicate the availability of the pie with meat in the Slow Cooker.

Buns

Ingredients:
- 2 cups of flour
- 2/3 cup of milk
- 3 tablespoons sugar
- 3 tablespoons butter
- 1 egg
- 2 tablespoons orange juice
- 1 teaspoon dried yeast
- salt, vanilla sugar

Preparation:
1. Dissolve the yeast in warm milk.
2. Sift flour, add salt and orange juice.
3. Egg, sugar, vanilla sugar and melted butter mix and add to the flour, leaving 2 tablespoons to lubricate the rolls.
4. Combine the flour with the milk-yeast mixture and knead the dough.
5. Cover it and put it in a warm place.
6. Then we form buns. If they are without a filling, then simply roll the ball. If the filling, then from a piece of dough to form a cake. We put the stuffing on the cake and wrap it.
7. Grease the pan with butter and place the buns with a seam on the bottom. And give a go.
8. Put on "Heating" and leave for half an hour. Then she smeared the buns with the mixture we left: egg + sugar + butter.
9. Bake in "Baking" mode for 60 minutes.

Cupcake with frozen blueberries and nuts

Ingredients:
- 75 g of softened margarine
- 1/2 cup warm milk
- 2 eggs
- 2 1/2 glasses of plain flour
- 1 cup of sugar
- 2 1/2 teaspoons baking powder
- 1/2 teaspoon soda
- 1 teaspoon of salt
- 1 glass of frozen blueberries or blueberries
- 1/2 cup chopped walnuts
- 1/2 teaspoon grated lemon peel

Preparation:
1. Frozen berries thaw, when thawed, drain excess liquid.
2. In a bowl, whip the soft margarine, milk, eggs and sugar. Add flour, baking powder, soda and salt. Gently add berries, nuts and zest. Mix gently.
3. In the bread maker: Lubricate the bucket for the bread maker. Put the dough in a bucket, turn on the machine in the "Cupcake" mode and click Start. Fully cool in the bread maker before you remove it.
4. In the multivariate: The oven in the Baking mode 45 minutes, then leave for an hour in the heating mode.

Curd cake

Ingredients:
- 3 eggs
- 1 cup of sugar
- 150 g of butter
- 250 g cottage cheese
- 2 tablespoons sour cream
- 1 teaspoon baking powder
- 2 cups of flour

Preparation:
1. Eggs beat well with sugar, add butter. Cottage cheese rub through a sieve, add sour cream. To the cottage cheese add eggs with sugar and butter and whip until smooth.
2. Sift flour with baking powder and add to the cottage cheese mass. Mix well, place in a saucepan Slow Cooker, oiled.
3. We put on "Baking" for 1 hour, then for another 30 minutes. Since in Slow Cooker of different volume heating different, it may take more time or less time.

Orange pie in the Slow Cooker

Ingredients:
- 4 eggs
- 1 cup of sugar
- 1.5 cups of flour
- 1-2 tsp orange peel
- 2 oranges
- 1 teaspoon baking powder
- 2 kiwis for decoration

Preparation:
1. Mix all the ingredients and put them into the Slow Cooker.
2. Close the lid and cook in "Baking" mode.
3. Turn on the plate with the back side and decorate with kiwi slices.

Cottage cheese casserole with berries

Ingredients:
- 400 g cottage cheese
- 1/2 cup sugar
- a pinch of salt
- 3 eggs
- 3 tablespoons of semolina
- 1 bag of vanillin
- 0.5 teaspoon soda
- 1 teaspoon lemon zest
- 200 g of frozen berries
- 1 tablespoon butter

Preparation:
1. Eggs beat up with sugar and a pinch of salt in a lush light mass with a mixer. Add the cottage cheese, mix. Add mango, vanilla, zest and soda, leave for 10 minutes stand.
2. Oil the cup of the Slow Cooker. Put the cottage cheese mass on top of the berries. Put in the "Baking" mode for 1 hour.

Pancakes

Ingredients:
- 3 eggs
- 1/2 teaspoons of salt
- 3 tablespoons sugar
- 2 cups of milk
- 1 glass of water
- 2 cups of flour
- 2 tablespoons butter
- oil for frying

Preparation:
1. Beat eggs with salt and sugar, add milk, water. Stir and gradually pour in the flour. It is better to beat with a mixer, so the dough will be more homogeneous. Add the melted butter, mix.
2. Slow Cooker included in the "Baking" mode, give a good heat about 5 -7 minutes. Lubricate the bowl of Slow Cooker oil.
3. Pour the pancake batter with a thin layer on the bottom of the heated bowl. Fry for about 3 minutes, on each side with an open lid. Fry until the dough runs out. Finished pancakes can be served with sour cream, jam or other fillings.

Casserole with spinach and cottage cheese

Ingredients:
- 300 g of spinach ice cream
- bunch of green onions
- 4 eggs
- 400 g cottage cheese
- 2 cups of grated cheese
- salt pepper

Preparation:
1. Preheat the oven to 170 degrees. Lightly grease the baking dish.
2. Thaw the defrosted spinach in a saucepan, cook over medium heat, stirring, until softening, about 5 minutes. Drain and wring out the liquid. Add chopped green onions, lightly beaten eggs, cottage cheese and grated cheese. Salt-pepper to taste. Put into a baking dish.
3. Bake without covering in the oven at 170 degrees 45 minutes. Remove from oven and sprinkle with crumbs from crackers. Return to the oven and cook for another 15 minutes, or until the omelet becomes dense in consistency.

Cheesecake with blueberries

Ingredients:
- 100 g of butter
- 2 tablespoons of sugar
- 2 cups cookie crumbs
- 400 g of cream cheese
- 100 g of powdered sugar
- 4 eggs
- 50 g of blueberries
- 150 g of blueberry jam or jam

Preparation:
1. Melt the butter with sugar in the heating mode, pour into a bowl.
2. Wash the bowl and dry it, place in the bowl a silicone shape of the appropriate diameter.
3. In a bowl of butter and sugar, pour out the breadcrumbs of the pastry, mix well.
4. In the form put the resulting mass and evenly distribute the entire surface. Press it with your hand.
5. In a bowl, mix the softened cream cheese with sugar powder, one by one to beat the eggs, stirring after each. All stir until homogeneous. Add berries of blueberries, gently stir, do not whisk, trying not to press berries.
6. Pour the resulting mass into a mold in circular motions, starting from the middle.
7. Close the lid and bake in the Baking mode 45 minutes, after the signal turn off the mode and leave the cheesecake for 60 minutes cool in the Slow Cooker.
8. After this, hold a spatula or culinary knife or a thin wooden spatula along the edge of the mold so that when cooling the edges do not crack.
9. Carefully remove the shape from the bowl, top with blueberry jam or jam.
10. Remove the cheesecake for complete cooling in the refrigerator for the night or for 5-6 hours.

Pineapple cake

Ingredients:
- 200 g of butter
- 150 g of sugar
- 250 g of flour
- 3 eggs
- 10 g of a baking powder
- 1 packet of vanilla sugar
- 1 jar of pineapple

Preparation:
1. Melt the butter. Add sugar, eggs and vanillin. All the whip.
2. Then gradually introduce flour and baking powder. Knead the dough.
3. Lubricate the bowl with oil, sprinkle the bottom with sugar. Lay out the pineapple rings. Top with pour the dough.
4. We bake a pie in the Slow Cooker 65 minutes.

Banana Cake

Ingredients:
- 100 g of butter
- 2 eggs
- 2 cups of flour
- 1 cup of sugar
- 2 teaspoons baking powder
- 1 teaspoon of vanilla sugar
- a pinch of salt
- 2 bananas
- 100 ml of milk

Preparation:
1. Mix flour with baking powder and salt.
2. Mash bananas with a fork. Melt the butter. Add to the bananas. Also add eggs and sugar. All mix well.
3. Pour in the milk and vanilla. Mix again until homogeneity.
4. Pour in the flour, mix well.
5. Put it in the Slow Cooker, put it in "baking" mode for 1 hour and 20 minutes.

Pie with cranberries in a multicrew

Ingredients:
- 0.5 cups of sugar
- 50 g of butter
- 1 cup of cranberry
- 0.5 cup chopped nuts
- 100 g of butter
- 3/4 cup sugar
- 2 eggs
- 1 teaspoon vanilla
- 1 glass of sour cream
- 1.5 cups of flour
- 1 teaspoon baking powder
- 1 teaspoon soda
- 1/2 teaspoons ground cinnamon
- 1/4 teaspoons of salt

Preparation:
1. Turn the Slow Cooker heater on and melt the oil in it. Add the sugar and mix well with a spatula. The oil should not float separately but become a homogeneous gruel with sugar. Add the cranberries and nuts, mix and distribute evenly.
2. Sift into a separate bowl of flour, baking powder, soda, cinnamon and salt. Set it aside.
3. In a large bowl, beat the softened butter and 3/4 cup sugar. Eat eggs one at a time, then add vanilla. Then add flour mixture alternately with sour cream. Put the dough in a Slow Cooker over cranberries and nuts.
4. Put in the baking mode for 1 hour. Check the availability of a toothpick. If it comes out dry - gently turn the cake upside down on a serving dish. Cranberries with nuts will be on top. If part of the cranberries remains at the bottom of the Slow Cooker - spread, it over the pie.

Cake with strawberries

Ingredients:
- Eggs - 2 pieces
- Sugar - 200 g
- Sour cream - 5 tablespoons
- Butter - 100 g
- Vegetable oil - 5 tablespoons
- Flour 300 g
- Vanillin - 2 pieces
- Strawberries - 3 cups
- Sugar powder - 100 g

Preparation:
1. Pour 2 eggs and 200 grams of sugar into the container.
2. Whisk the eggs with sugar and add 5 tablespoons of sour cream, beat again.
3. Add the melted butter and vanillin, mix.
4. Now add the sifted flour.
5. The resulting mass should be beaten with a mixer until a homogeneous mass is obtained. The density should go out like sour cream.
6. Cover the baking paper on the bottom of the multiquark bowl.
7. Lubricate the bowl Slow Cooker and baking paper with vegetable oil. Put the dough, evenly spreading on the bottom.
8. Roll the strawberries in the sugar powder and lay them on the top of the dough in random order. Bake in the "Baking" mode for 70 minutes.
9. Gently remove the finished pie on the plate, remove the paper.
10. Top with powdered sugar.

Apple-honey cake

Ingredients:
- 1 kg of apples
- 3/4 cup vegetable oil
- 3 tablespoons honey
- 1 teaspoon cinnamon
- 1 1 \ 4 cups of sugar
- 4 eggs
- 2 1/2 cups of flour
- 1 tablespoon lemon zest
- 3 tablespoons sugar
- 1 teaspoon cinnamon

Preparation:
1. Peel the apples and cut each halve into another 8 pieces, fry the pieces in butter 5 minutes over a large fire. We add honey and cinnamon. Fry apples until golden brown.
2. Put sugar and butter in a bowl and whisk for 5 minutes. We add eggs and flour. Beat another 3 minutes. Add apples and lemon peel and mix well.
3. Pour into the mold and top with the sugar and cinnamon. We bake for 40 minutes.

Lemon cake

Ingredients:
- butter 150 g
- sugar 150 g
- wheat flour 210 g
- eggs 4 pieces
- lemon 1 piece
- baking powder 1 teaspoon
- raisins 50 g

Preparation:
Grate the lemon zest on a small grater with a whole lemon. Rinse the zest with a sugar fork to saturate the cake with a lemon flavor. Add soft butter, grate. Beat with a mixer. Add the baking powder for the dough and gradually add the flour without stopping whipping with a mixer. After the dough is well mixed, add the raisins and stir with a spoon. Lubricate the baking dish with butter. Bake in Slow Cooker in Baking mode 50 minutes. In the oven, bake for 20 minutes at a temperature of 180 degrees. Decorate the finished cupcake with powdered sugar.

Coconut cake

Ingredients:
- Flour - 400 g
- Butter - 250 g
- Egg - 5 pieces
- Sugar - 200 g
- Milk - 125 liters
- Chocolate - 250 g
- Baking Powder - 1 teaspoon
- Vanilla sugar - 15 g

Preparation:
1. In the softened butter add sugar, vanilla sugar and whisk at low speed mixer to the state of white cream
2. One by one add all the eggs to the oil mixture each time with a little whisking mixer at the lowest speed.
3. Sifted flour mixed with baking powder and, in small portions, add to the egg-oil mixture, each time stirring well with a spatula.
4. Add milk at room temperature and mix the dough well.
5. Chocolate is broken into pieces and added to the dough. We mix it.
6. We will lubricate the cup of MV with a small amount of vegetable oil and lay out the dough.
7. We select the "Baking" mode, we set the time - 1 hour 5 minutes. At the end of the program, leave the cupcake in the "Heating" mode for 20 minutes.
8. We pull out the cupcake with the help of a bowl for steaming and let the cupcake completely cool.
9. Sprinkle the top with coconut chips.

Copyright: Published in the United States by Teresa Moore / © Teresa Moore All Rights Reserved. No part of this publication or the information in it may be quoted from or reproduced in any form by means such as printing, scanning, photocopying or otherwise without prior written permission of the copyright holder. Disclaimer and Terms of Use: Effort has been made to ensure that the information in this book is accurate and complete, however, the author and the publisher do not warrant the accuracy of the information, text and graphics contained within the book due to the rapidly changing nature of science, research, known and unknown facts and internet. The Author and the publisher do not hold any responsibility for errors, omissions or contrary interpretation of the subject matter herein. This book is presented solely for motivational and informational purposes only.

Printed in Great Britain
by Amazon